THE APOLOGY OF SOCRATES

&

THE CRITO

by

Plato

the 1864 translation of

Benjamin Jowett

BANDANNA BOOKS 1993 SANTA BARBARA

LITTLE HUMANIST CLASSICS

n o n s e x i s t • s e c u l a r

1. *I Ching*, tr. Asa Bonnershaw, with Confucius' own notes
2. *Sappho*, tr. N. Browne. All the extant poems. Illustrated by Jeanne Morgan.
3. *The Little Gospel*, Leo Tolstoy, tr. Anne W. Basshorn. With Tolstoy's anti-church introduction.
4. *Letters on the Gita*, Mohandas K. Gandhi's exposition of the Bhagavad Gita
5. *Areopagitica*, John Milton. The nonpareil defense of freedom of the press.
6. *The Apology & Crito*, Plato, in Benjamin Jowett's original lively translation
7. *Ghazals*, Ghalib, tr. from the Urdu by Basho Swanner
8. *Original Leaves of Grass*, Walt Whitman. The 1855 edition, with the essay "America."

also of interest from Bandanna Books

John Wesley's *Short Latin Grammar.*
A Cretan Cycle: Fragments from Knossos (poems), Marilyn Coffey, illustrated by Kostas Lekakis

ISBN 0-942208-05-6 • LC 86-064057

EDITOR'S NOTE

BENJAMIN JOWETT'S original translation of the Apology is remarkably free from Victorianisms, and brings to life the figure of Socrates with an easy colloquialism. Later in his career, Jowett decided that some of his own easiness of translation was simply inaccuracy, and he replaced the flow of speech with a more literal rendering. My own paradigm in each of the translations in the Little Humanist Classics series is to imagine the author humself watching over the translator's shoulder. If Plato were writing in American English, how would he have said it? In the case of Plato, we are confronted with a man who more or less invented a literary form—the dialogue—for putting complex ideas into popular form; in other words, making the metaphysical pill easy to swallow. Following this line of reasoning, we have chosen to republish the younger Jowett, a man remarkably close in spirit to Plato. How close to the true spirit of Socrates he has come is a moot point. I.F. Stone's recent *The Trial of Socrates* suggests that there was Plato's Socrates, Xenophon's Socrates, Aristophanes' Socrates—and then there was the stonemason who walked about Athens, and left no writings behind, just some sparks in human souls.

One other editorial matter needs mentioned here. In keeping with BBooks' project of humanizing the classics, we have used humanist pronouns in this book to refer to a third person generally, without reference to sex. *Hu, hus, hum* are pronounced exactly the same as the indefinite pronoun set *who, whose, whom. Humself* and other nonsexist words are also used in the appropriate places. I believe that Plato looking over my shoulder would approve.

A. S. Ash
Jan. 1992

THE APOLOGY

Hᴏᴡ ʏᴏᴜ ʜᴀᴠᴇ ꜰᴇʟᴛ, ᴏ ᴀᴛʜᴇɴɪᴀɴꜱ, at hearing the speeches of my accusers, I cannot tell; but I know that their persuasive words almost made me forget who I was, such was the effect of them; and yet they have hardly spoken a word of truth. But many as their falsehoods were, there was one of them which quite amazed me: I mean when they told you to be upon your guard, and not to let yourselves be deceived by the force of my eloquence. They ought to have been ashamed of saying this, because they were sure to be detected as soon as I opened my lips and displayed my deficiency; they certainly did appear to be most shameless in saying this, unless by the force of eloquence they mean the force of truth; for then I do indeed admit that I am eloquent. But in how different a way from theirs! Well, as I was saying, they have hardly uttered a word, or not more than a word, of truth; but you shall hear from me the whole truth: not, however, delivered after their manner, in a set oration duly ornamented with words and phrases. No, indeed! but I shall use the words and arguments which occur to me at the moment; for I am certain that this is right, and that at my time of life I ought not to be appearing before you, O people of Athens, in the character of a juvenile orator: let no one expect this of me. And I must beg of you to grant me one favor, which is this—If you hear me using the same words in my defense which I have been in the habit of using, and which most of you may have heard in the agora, and at the tables of the money-changers, or anywhere else, I would ask you not to be surprised at this, and not to interrupt me. For I am more than seventy years of age, and this is the first time that I have ever appeared in a court of law, and I am quite a stranger to the ways of the place; and therefore I would have you regard me as if I were really a stranger, whom you would excuse if hu spoke in hus native tongue, and after the fashion of hus country: that I think is not an unfair request. Never mind the manner, which may or may not be good; but think only of the justice of my cause, and give heed to that: let the judge decide justly and the speaker speak truly.

And first, I have to reply to the older charges and to my first accusers, and then I will go on to the later ones. For I have had many accusers, who accused me of old, and their false charges have continued during many years; and I am more afraid of them than of Anytus and his associates, who are dangerous, too, in their own way.

9

But far more dangerous are these, who began when you were children, and took possession of your minds with their falsehoods, telling of one Socrates, a wise man, who speculated about the heaven above, and searched into the earth beneath, and made the worse appear the better cause. These are the accusers whom I dread; for they are the circulators of this rumor, and their hearers are too apt to fancy that speculators of this sort do not believe in the gods. And they are many, and their charges against me are of ancient date, and they made them in days when you were impressible—in childhood, or perhaps in youth—and the cause when heard went by default, for there was none to answer. And hardest of all, their names I do not know and cannot tell; unless in the chance case of a comic poet [*Aristophanes*]. But the main body of these slanderers who from envy and malice have wrought upon you—and there are some of them who are convinced themselves, and impart their convictions to others—all these, I say, are most difficult to deal with; for I cannot have them up here, and examine them, and therefore I must simply fight with shadows in my own defense, and examine when there is no one who answers. I will ask you then to assume with me, as I was saying, that my opponents are of two kinds—one recent, the other ancient; and I hope that you will see the propriety of my answering the latter first, for these accusations you heard long before the others, and much oftener.

Well, then, I will make my defense, and I will endeavor in the short time which is allowed to do away with this evil opinion of me which you have held for such a long time and I hope that I may succeed, if this be well for you and me and that my words may find favor with you. But I know that to accomplish this is not easy—I quite see the nature of the task. Let the event be as God wills: in obedience to the law I make my defense.

I will begin at the beginning, and ask what the accusation is which has given rise to this slander of me, and which has encouraged Meletus to proceed against me. What do the slanderers say? They shall be my prosecutors, and I will sum up their words in an affidavit: *Socrates is an evil-doer, and a curious person, who searches into things under the earth and in heaven, and he makes the worse appear the better cause; and he teaches the aforesaid doctrines to others.* That is the nature of the accusation, and that is what you have seen yourselves in the comedy of Aristophanes, who has introduced a man whom he calls Socrates, going about and saying that he can walk in the air, and talking a deal of nonsense concerning matters of which I do not pretend to know either much or little—not that I mean to say anything disparaging of anyone who is a student of natural philosophy. I should be very sorry if Meletus could lay that to my charge. But the simple truth is, O Athenians, that I have nothing to do with these studies. Very many of those here present are witnesses to the truth of this, and to them I appeal. Speak then, you who have heard me, and tell your neighbors whether any of you have ever known me hold forth in few words or in many upon matters of this sort. . . . You hear their answer. And from what they say of this you will be able to judge of the truth of the rest.

As little foundation is there for the report that I am a teacher, and take money; that is no more true than the other. Although, if a man is able to teach, I honor him for being paid. There is Gorgias of Leontium, and Prodicus of Ceos, and Hippias of Elis, who go the round of the cities, and are able to persuade the young men to leave their own citizens, by whom they might be taught for nothing, and come to them, whom they not only pay, but are thankful if they may be allowed to pay them. There is actually a Parian philosopher residing in Athens, of whom I have heard; and I came to hear of him in this way: I met a man who has spent a world of money on the Sophists, Callias the son of Hipponicus, and knowing that he had sons, I asked him:

"Callias," I said, "if your two sons were foals or calves, there would be no difficulty in finding someone to put over them; we should hire a trainer of horses, or a farmer probably, who would improve and perfect them in their own proper virtue and excellence; but as they are human beings, whom are you thinking of placing over them? Is there anyone who understands human and political virtue? You must have thought about this, as you have sons; is there anyone?"

"There is," he said.

"Who is he?" said I, "and of what country? and what does he charge?"

"Evenus the Parian," he replied, "he is the man, and his charge is five minae."

Happy is Evenus, I said to myself, *if he really has this wisdom, and teaches at such a modest charge.* Had I the same, I should have been very proud and conceited; but the truth is that I have no knowledge of the kind, O Athenians.

I dare say that someone will ask the question, *Why is this, Socrates, and what is the origin of these accusations of you: for there must have been something strange which you have been doing? All this great fame and talk about you would never have arisen if you had been like other people: tell us, then, why this is, as we should be sorry to judge hastily of you.*

teaching is valuable as is learning.

11

Now, I regard this as a fair challenge, and I will endeavor to explain to you the origin of this name of "wise," and of this evil fame. Please to attend, then. And although some of you may think that I am joking, I declare that I will tell you the entire truth.

People of Athens, this reputation of mine has come of a certain sort of wisdom which I possess. If you ask me what kind of wisdom, I reply, such wisdom as is by human, for to that extent I am inclined to believe that I am wise; whereas the persons of whom I was speaking have a superhuman wisdom, which I may fail to describe, because I have it not myself; and hu who says that I have, speaks falsely, and is taking away my character.

And here, O people of Athens, I must beg you not to interrupt me, even if I seem to say something extravagant. For the word which I will speak is not mine. I will refer you to a witness who is worthy of credit, and will tell you about my wisdom—whether I have any, and of what sort—and that witness shall be the god of Delphi.

You must have known Chaerephon; he was early a friend of mine, and also a friend of yours, for he shared in the recent exile of the people, and returned with you. Well, Chaerephon, as you know, was very impetuous in all his doings, and he went to Delphi and boldly asked the oracle to tell him whether—as I was saying, I must beg you not to interrupt—he asked the oracle to tell him whether there was anyone wiser than I was, and the Pythian prophetess answered that there was no man wiser. Chaerephon is dead himself; but his brother, who is in court, will confirm the truth of this story.

Why do I mention this? Because I am going to explain to you why I have such an evil name. When I heard the answer, I said to myself, *What can the god mean? and what is the interpretation of this riddle? for I know that I have no wisdom, small or great. What can hu mean when hu says that I am the wisest of persons? And yet hu is a god, and cannot lie; that would be against hus nature.*

After a long consideration, I at last thought of a method of trying the question. I reflected that if I could only find a person wiser than myself, then I might go to the god with a refutation in my hand. I should say to hum, *Here is a person who is wiser than I am; but you said that I was the wisest.*

Accordingly I went to one who had the reputation of wisdom, and observed hum—hus name I need not mention; hu was a politician whom I selected for examination—and the result was as follows: When I began to talk with hum, I could not help thinking that hu was not really wise, although hu was thought wise by many, and wiser still by humself; and I went and tried to explain to hum that hu thought humself wise, but was not really wise; and the consequence was that hu hated me, and hus enmity was shared by several who were present and heard me.

So I left hum, saying to myself, as I went away: Well, although I do not suppose that either of us knows anything really beautiful and good, I am better off than hu is—for hu knows nothing, and thinks that hu knows; I neither know nor think that I know. In this latter particular, then, I seem to have slightly the advantage of hum.

Then I went to another who had still higher philosophical pretensions, and my conclusion was exactly the same. I made another enemy of hum, and of many others besides hum.

After this I went to one person after another, being not unconscious of the enmity which I provoked, and I lamented and feared this: but necessity was laid upon me—the word of God, I thought, ought to be considered first. And I said to myself, *Go I must to all who appear to know, and find out the meaning of the oracle.* And I swear to you, Athenians, by the dog I swear!—for I must tell you the truth—the result of my mission was just this: I found that the people most in repute were all but the most foolish; and that some inferior people were really wiser and better. *Those who are wise are humble.*

I will tell you the tale of my wanderings and of the "Herculean" labors, as I may call them, which I endured only to find at last the oracle irrefutable. When I left the politicians, I went to the poets; tragic, dithyrambic, and all sorts. And there, I said to myself, you will be detected; now you will find out that you are more ignorant than they are.

Accordingly I took them some of the most elaborate passages in their own writings, and asked what was the meaning of them—thinking that they would teach me something. Will you believe me? I am almost ashamed to speak of this, but still I must say that there is hardly a person present who would not have talked better about their poetry than they did themselves. That showed me in an instant that not by wisdom do poets write poetry, but by a sort of genius and inspiration; they are like diviners or soothsayers who also say many fine things, but do not understand the meaning of them. And the poets appeared to me to be much in the same case; and I further observed that upon the strength of their poetry they believed themselves to be the wisest of people in other things in which they were not wise. So I departed, conceiving myself to be superior to them for the same reason that I was superior to the politicians.

At last I went to the artisans, for I was conscious that I knew nothing at all, as I may say, and I was sure that they knew many

poets create spectacle — not humble

fine things; and here I was not mistaken, for they did know many things of which I was ignorant, and in this they certainly were wiser than I was. But I observed that even the good artisans fell into the same error as the poets—because they were good workmen they thought that they also knew all sorts of high matters, and this defect in them overshadowed their wisdom—therefore I asked myself on behalf of the oracle, whether I would like to be as I was, neither having their knowledge nor their ignorance, or like them in both; and I made answer to myself and the oracle that I was better off as I was.

This investigation has led to my having many enemies of the worst and most dangerous kind, and has given occasion also to many calumnies. And I am called wise, for my hearers always imagine that I myself possess the wisdom which I find wanting in others: but the truth is, O people of Athens, that God only is wise; and in this oracle hu intends to say that human wisdom is worth little or nothing; hu is not speaking of Socrates, hu is only using my name as an illustration, as if hu said, *Hu, O people, is the wisest, who, like Socrates, knows that hus wisdom is in truth worth nothing.*

And so I go my way, obedient to the god, and search and make inquisition into the wisdom of anyone, whether citizen or stranger, who appears to be wise; and if hu is not wise, then in vindication of the oracle I show hum that hu is not wise; and this occupation quite absorbs me, and I have no time to give either to any public matter of interest or to any concern of my own, but I am in utter poverty by reason of my devotion to the god.

There is another thing—young men of the richer classes, who have not much to do, come about me of their own accord; they like to hear the pretenders examined, and they often imitate me, and examine others themselves; there are plenty of persons, as they soon enough discover, who think that they know something, but really know little or nothing; and then those who are examined by them instead of being angry with themselves are angry with me: *This confounded Socrates,* they say, *this villainous misleader of youth!*—and then if somebody asks them, *Why, what evil does he practice or teach?* they do not know, and cannot tell; but in order that they may not appear to be at a loss, they repeat the ready-made charges which are used against all philosophers about teaching things up in the clouds and under the earth, and having no gods, and making the worse appear the better cause; for they do not like to confess that their pretense of knowledge has been detected—which is the truth; and as they are numerous and ambitious and energetic, and are all in battle array and have persuasive tongues, they have filled your ears with their loud and inveterate calumnies.

And this is the reason why my three accusers, Meletus and Anytus and Lycon, have set upon me; Meletus, who has a quarrel with me on behalf of the poets; Anytus, on behalf of the craftspeople; Lycon, on behalf of the rhetoricians. And, as I said at the beginning, I cannot expect to get rid of this mass of calumny all in a moment.

And this, O people of Athens, is the truth and the whole truth; I have concealed nothing, I have dissembled nothing. And yet, I know that this plainness of speech makes them hate me, and what is their hatred but a proof that I am speaking the truth?—this is the occasion and reason of their slander against me, as you will find out either in this or in any future enquiry.

I have said enough in my defense against the first class of my accusers; I turn to the second class who are headed by Meletus, that good and patriotic man, as he calls himself. And now I will try to defend myself against them: these new accusers must also have their affidavit read. What do they say? Something of this sort: *That Socrates is a doer of evil, and corrupter of the youth; and he does not believe in the gods of the state, and has other new divinities of his own.* That is the sort of charge; and now let us examine the particular counts. He says that I am a doer of evil, who corrupt the youth; but I say, people of Athens, that Meletus is a doer of evil, and the evil is that he makes a joke of a serious matter, and is to ready at bringing other people to trial from a pretended zeal and interest about matters in which he really never had the smallest interest. And the truth of this I will endeavor to prove to you.

Come here, Meletus, and let me ask a question of you. You think a great deal about the improvement of youth?

Yes, I do.

Tell the judges, then, who is their improver; for you must know, as you have taken the pains to discover their corrupter, and are citing and accusing me before them. Speak, then, and tell the judges who their improver is. Observe, Meletus, that you are silent, and have nothing to say. But is not this rather disgraceful, and a very considerable proof of what I was saying, that you have no interest in the matter? Speak up, friend, and tell us who their improver is.

The laws.

But that, my good sir, is not my meaning. I want to know who the person is, who, in the first place, knows the laws.

The judges, Socrates, who are present in court.

What, do you mean to say, Meletus, that they are able to instruct and improve youth?

Certainly they are.

What, all of them, or some only and not others?

All of them.

By the goddess Hera, that is good news! There are plenty of improvers, then. And what do you say of the audience—do they improve them?

Yes, they do.

And the senators?

Yes, the senators improve them.

But perhaps the ecclesiasts corrupt them?—or do they too improve them?

They improve them.

Then every Athenian improves and elevates them; all with the exception of myself; and I alone am their corrupter? Is that what you affirm?

That is what I stoutly affirm.

I am very unfortunate if that is true. But suppose I ask you a question: Would you say that this also holds true in the case of horses? Does one person do them harm and all the world good? Is not the exact opposite of this true? One person is able to do them good, or at least not many; the trainer of horses, that is to say, does them good, and others who have to do with them rather injure them? Is not that true, Meletus, of horses, or of any other animals? Yes, certainly. Whether you or Anytus say yes or no, that is no matter. Happy indeed would be the condition of youth if they had one corrupter only, and all the rest of the world were their improvers. And you, Meletus, have sufficiently shown that you never had a thought about the young; your carelessness is seen in your not caring about the matters spoken of in this very indictment.

And now, Meletus, I must ask you another question: Which is better, to live among bad citizens, or among good ones? Answer, friend, I say; for that is a question is one which may be easily answered. Do not the good do their neighbors good, and the bad do them evil?

Certainly.

And is there anyone who would rather be injured than benefited by those who live with hum? Answer, my good friend, the law requires you to answer—does anyone like to be injured?

Certainly not.

And when you accuse me of corrupting and deteriorating

the youth, do you allege that I corrupt them intentionally or unintentionally?

Intentionally, I say.

But you have just admitted that the good do their neighbors good, and the evil do them evil. Now, is that a truth which your superior wisdom has recognized thus early in life, and am I, at my age, in such darkness and ignorance as not to know that if a person with whom I have to live is corrupted by me, I am very likely to be harmed by hum, and yet I corrupt hum, and intentionally, too; that is what you are saying, and of that you will never persuade me or any other human being. But either I do not corrupt them, or I corrupt them unintentionally, so that on either view of the case you lie. If my offense is unintentional, the law has no cognizance of unintentional offenses: you ought to have taken me privately, and warned and admonished me; for if I had been better advised, I should have left off doing what I only did unintentionally—no doubt I should; whereas you hated to converse with me or teach me, but you indicted me in this court, which is a place not of instruction, but of punishment.

I have shown, Athenians, as I was saying, that Meletus has no care at all, great or small, about the matter. But still I should like to know, Meletus, in what I am affirmed to corrupt the young. I suppose you mean, as I infer from your indictment, that I teach them not to acknowledge the gods which the state acknowledges, but some other new divinities or spiritual agencies in their stead. These are the lessons which corrupt the youth, as you say.

Yes, that I say emphatically.

Then, by the gods, Meletus, of whom we are speaking, tell me and the court, in somewhat plainer terms, what you mean! for I do not as yet understand whether you affirm that I teach others to acknowledge some gods, and therefore do believe in gods and am not an entire atheist—this you do not lay to my charge—but only that they are not the same gods which the city recognizes—the charge is that they are different gods. Or, do you mean that I am an atheist simply, and a teacher of atheism?

I mean the latter—that you are a complete atheist.

That is an extraordinary statement, Meletus. Why do you say that? Do you mean that I do not believe in the godhead of the sun or moon, which is the common creed of all people?

I assure you, judges, that he does not believe in them; for he says that the sun is stone, and the moon earth.

Friend Meletus, you think that you are accusing Anaxagoras: and you have but a bad opinion of the judges, if you fancy them ignorant to such a degree as not to know that these doctrines are found in the books of Anaxagoras the Clazomenian, who is full of them. And these are the doctrines which the youth are said to learn of Socrates, when there are not unfrequently exhibitions of them at the theater (price of admission one drachma at the most); and they might cheaply purchase them, and laugh at Socrates if he pretends to father such eccentricities. And so, Meletus, you really think that I do not believe in any god?

I swear by Zeus that you believe absolutely in none at all.

You are a liar, Meletus, not believed even by yourself. I cannot help thinking, people of Athens, that Meletus is reckless and impudent, and that he has written this indictment in a spirit of mere wantonness and youthful bravado. Has he not compounded a riddle, thinking to try me? He said to himself: *I shall see whether this wise Socrates will discover my ingenious contradiction, or whether I shall be able to deceive him and the rest of them.* For he certainly does appear to me to contradict himself in the indictment as much as if he said that Socrates is guilty of not believing in the gods, and yet of believing in them—but this is surely a piece of fun.

I should like you, O people of Athens, to join me in examining what I conceive to be his inconsistency; and do you, Meletus, answer. And I must remind you that you are not to interrupt if I speak in my accustomed manner:

Did ever a person, Meletus, believe in the existence of human things, and not of human beings? . . . I wish, people of Athens, that he would answer, and not be always trying to get up an interruption. Did ever anyone believe in horsemanship, and not in horses? or in flute-playing, and not in flute-players? No, my friend; I will answer to you and to the court, as you refuse to answer for yourself. There is no one who ever did. But now please to answer the next question: Can a person believe in spiritual and divine agencies, and not in spirits or demigods?

Hu cannot.

I am glad that I have extracted that answer, by the assistance of the court; nevertheless you swear in the indictment that I teach and believe in divine or spiritual agencies (new or old, no matter for that); at any rate, I believe in spiritual agencies, as you say and swear in the affidavit; but if I believe in divine beings, I must believe in spirits or demigods; is not that true? Yes, that is true, for I may assume that your silence gives assent to that. Now what are spirits or demigods? are they not either gods or the children of gods? Is that true?

Yes, that is true.

But this is just the ingenious riddle of which I was speaking: the demigods or spirits are gods, and you say first that I don't believe in gods, and then again that I do believe in gods; that is, if I believe in demigods. For if the demigods are the illegitimate children of gods, whether by the nymphs or by any other mothers, as is thought, that, as all will allow, necessarily implies the existence of their parents. You might as well affirm the existence of mules, and deny that of horses and asses.

Such nonsense, Meletus, could only have been intended by you as a trial of me. You have put this into the indictment because you had nothing real of which to accuse me. But no one who has a particle of understanding will ever be convinced by you that the same people can believe in divine and superhuman things, and yet not believe that there are gods and demigods and heroes.

I have said enough in answer to the charge of Meletus: any elaborate defense is unnecessary; but as I was saying before, I certainly have many enemies, and this is what will be my destruction if I am destroyed; of that I am certain; not Meletus, nor yet Anytus, but the envy and detraction of the world, which has been the death of many good people, and will probably be the death of many more; there is no danger of my being the last of them.

Someone will say: *And are you not ashamed, Socrates, of a course of life which is likely to bring you to an untimely end?* To hum I may fairly answer: There you are mistaken: a person who is good for anything ought not to calculate the chance of living or dying; hu ought only to consider whether in doing anything hu is doing right or wrong—acting the part of a good person or of a bad.

Whereas, upon your view, the heroes who fell at Troy were not good for much, and the son of Thetis above all, who altogether despised danger in comparison with disgrace; and when his goddess mother said to him, in his eagerness to slay Hector, that if he avenged his companion Patroclus, and slew Hector, he would die himself—"Fate," as she said, "waits upon you next after Hector"; he, hearing this, utterly despised danger and death, and instead of fearing them, feared rather to live in dishonor, and not to avenge his friend. "Let me die next," he replies, "and be avenged of my enemy, rather than abide here by the beaked ships, a scorn and a burden of the earth."

Had Achilles any thought of death and danger? For wherever a person's place is, whether the place which hu has chosen or that in which hu has been placed by a commander, there hu ought to remain in the hour of danger; hu should not think of death, or of anything, but of disgrace. And this, O people of Athens, is a true saying.

Strange, indeed, would be my conduct, O people of Athens, if I, who, when I was ordered by the generals whom you chose to command me at Potidaea and Amphipolis and Delium, remained where they placed me, like any other soldier, facing death—if, I say, now, when, as I conceive and imagine, God orders me to fulfill the philosopher's mission of searching into myself and other people, I were to desert my post through fear of death, or any other fear; that would indeed be strange, and I might justly be arraigned in court for denying the existence of the gods, if I disobeyed the oracle because I was afraid of death: then I should be fancying that I was wise when I was not wise. For this fear of death is indeed the pretense of wisdom, and not real wisdom, being the appearance of knowing the unknown; since no one knows whether death, which they in their fear apprehend to be the greatest evil, may not be the greatest good. Is there not here conceit of knowledge, which is a disgraceful sort of ignorance? And this is the point in which, as I think, I am superior to people in general, and in which I might perhaps fancy myself wiser than other people—that whereas I know but little of the world below, I do not suppose that I know: but I do know that injustice and disobedience to a better, whether God or human, is evil and dishonorable, and I will never fear or avoid a possible good rather than a certain evil.

And therefore, if you let me go now, and reject the counsels of Anytus, who said that if I were not put to death I ought not to have been prosecuted, and that if I escape now, your sons will all be utterly ruined by listening to my words—if you say to me, *Socrates, this time we will not mind Anytus, and will let you off, but upon one condition, that you are not to inquire and speculate in this way any more, and that if you are caught doing this again you shall die*—if this was the condition on which you let me go, I should reply: People of Athens, I honor and love you; but I shall obey God rather than you, and while I have life and strength I shall never cease from the practice and teaching of philosophy, exhorting anyone whom I meet after my manner, and convincing hum, saying: *O my friend, why do you, who are a citizen of the great and mighty and wise city of Athens, care so much about laying up the greatest amount of money and honor and reputation, and so little about wisdom and truth and the greatest improvement of the soul, which you never regard or heed at all? Are you not ashamed of this?*

And if the person with whom I am arguing, says: *Yes, but I do care,* I do not depart or let hum go at once; I interrogate and examine and cross-examine hum, and if I think that hu has no virtue, but only says that hu has, I reproach hum with undervaluing the greater, and overvaluing the less. And this I should say to everyone whom I meet, young and old, citizen and alien, but especially to the citizens, inasmuch as they are my brothers and sisters.

For this is the command to God, as I would have you know; and I believe that to this day no greater good has ever happened in the state than my service to the God. For I do nothing but go about persuading you all, old and young alike, not to take thought for your persons or your properties, but first and chiefly to care about the greatest improvement of the soul. I tell you that virtue is not given by money, but that from virtue come money and every other good of humanity, public as well as private.

This is my teaching, and if this is the doctrine which corrupts the youth, my influence is ruinous indeed. But if anyone says that this is not my teaching, hu is speaking an untruth. Wherefore, O people of Athens, I say to you, do as Anytus bids or not as Anytus bids, and either acquit me or not; but whatever you do, know that I shall never alter my ways, not even if I have to die many times.

People of Athens, do not interrupt, but hear me; there was an agreement between us that you should hear me out. And I have something more to say, at which you may be inclined to cry out; but I beg that you will not do this. I would have you know, that if you kill such a one as I am, you will injure yourselves more than you will injure me. Meletus and Anytus will not injure me: they cannot; for it is not in the nature of things that a bad person should injure a better than humself. I do not deny that hum may, perhaps, kill hum, or drive hum into exile, or deprive hum of civil rights; and he may imagine, and others may imagine, that hu is doing hum a great injury: but in that I do not agree with hum; for the evil of doing as Anytus is doing—of unjustly taking away another's life—is greater far.

And now, Athenians, I am not going to argue for my own sake, as you may think, but for yours, that you may not sin against the God, or lightly reject his boon by condemning me. For if you kill me you will not easily find another like me, who, if I may use such a ludicrous figure of speech, am a sort of gadfly, given to the state by the God; and the state is like a great and noble horse who is tardy in hus motions owing to hus very size, and requires to be stirred into life. I am that gadfly which God has given the state, and all day long and in all places am always fastening upon you, arousing and persuading and reproaching you.

And as you will not easily find another like me, I would advise you to spare me. I dare say that you may feel irritated at being suddenly awakened when you are caught napping; and you may think that if you were to strike me dead as Anytus advises, which you easily might, then you would sleep on for the remainder of your lives, unless God in hus care of you gives you another gadfly.

And that I am given to you by God is proved by this: that if I had been like other people, I should not have neglected all my own concerns, or patiently seen the neglect of them during all these years, and have been doing yours, coming to you individually, like a father or elder brother, exhorting you to regard virtue; this, I say, would not be like human nature. And had I gained anything, or if my exhortations had been paid, there would have been some sense in that: but now, as you will perceive, not even the impudence of my accusers dares to say that I have ever exacted or sought pay of anyone; they have no witness of that. And I have a witness of the truth of what I say; my poverty is a sufficient witness.

Someone may wonder why I go about in private, giving advice and busying myself with the concerns of others, but do not venture to come forward in public and advise the state. I will tell you the reason of this. You have often heard me speak of an oracle or sign which comes to me, and is the divinity which Meletus ridicules in the indictment. This sign I have had ever since I was a child. The sign is a voice which comes to me and always forbids me to do something which I am going to do, but never commands me to do anything, and this is what stands in the way of my being a politician. And rightly, as I think. For I am certain, O people of Athens, that if I had engaged in politics, I should have perished long ago, and done no good either to you or to myself. And don't be offended at my telling you the truth: for the truth is, that no one who goes to war with you or any other multitude, honestly struggling against the commission of unrighteousness and wrong in the state, will save hus life; hu who will really fight for the right, if hu would live even for a little while, must have a private station and not a public one.

I can give you as proofs of this, not words only, but deeds, which you value more than words. Let me tell you a passage of my own life, which will prove to you that I should never have yielded to injustice from any fear of death, and that if I had not yielded I should have died at once. I will tell you a story—tasteless, perhaps, and commonplace, but nevertheless true. The only office of state which I ever held, O people of Athens, was that of senator; the tribe Antiochis, which is my tribe, had the presidency at the trial of the generals who had not taken up the bodies of the slain after the battle of Arginusae; and you proposed to try them all together, which was illegal, as you all thought afterwards; but at the time I was the only one of the prytanes who was opposed to the illegality, and I gave my vote against you; and when the orators threatened to impeach and arrest me, and have me taken away, and you called and shouted, I made up my mind that I would run the risk, having law and justice with me, rather than take part in your injustice because I feared imprisonment and death. This happened in the days of the democracy.

But when the oligarchy of the Thirty was in power, they sent for me and four others into the rotunda, and bade us bring Leon the Salaminian from Salamis, as they wanted to execute him. This was a specimen of the sort of commands which they were always giving with the view of implicating as many as possible in their crimes; and then I showed, not in word only but in deed, that, if I may be allowed to use such an expression, I cared not a straw for death, and that my only fear was the fear of doing an unrighteous or unholy thing. For the strong arm of that oppressive power did not frighten me into doing wrong; and when we came out of the rotunda the other four went to Salamis and fetched Leon, but I went quietly home. For which I might have lost my life, had not the power of the Thirty shortly afterwards come to an end. And to this many will witness.

Now, do you really imagine that I could have survived all these years, if I had led a public life, supposing that like a good man I had always supported the right and had made justice, as I ought, the first thing? No indeed, people of Athens, neither I nor any other.

But I have been always the same in all my actions, public as well as private, and never have I yielded any base compliance to those who are slanderously termed my disciples, or to any other. For the truth is that I have no regular disciples: but if anyone likes to come and hear me while I am pursuing my mission, whether hu be young or old, hu may freely come. Nor do I converse with those who pay only, and not with those who do not pay; but anyone, whether hu be rich or poor, may ask and answer me and listen to my words; and whether hu turns out to be a bad person or a good one, that cannot be justly laid to my charge, as I never taught anything. And if anyone says that hu has ever learned or heard anything from me in private which all the world has not heard, I should like you to know that hu is speaking an untruth.

But I shall be asked, *Why do people delight in continually conversing with you?* I have told you already, Athenians, the whole truth about this: they like to hear the cross-examination of the pretenders to wisdom; there is amusement in it. And this is a duty which the God has imposed upon me, as I am assured by oracles, visions, and in every sort of way in which the will of divine power was ever signified to anyone.

This is true, O Athenians; or, if not true, would be soon refuted. For if I am really corrupting the youth, and have corrupted some of them already, those of them who have grown up and have become sensible that I gave them bad advice in the days of their youth should come forward as accusers, and take their revenge; and if they do not like to come themselves, some of their relatives, fathers, brothers, or other kinfolk, should say what evil their families have suffered at my hands. Now is their time.

Many of them I see in the court. There is Crito, who is of the same age and of the same deme with myself, and there is Critobulus his son, whom I also see. Then again there is Lysanias of Sphettus, who is the father of Aeschines—he is present; and also there is Antiphon of Cephisus, who is the father of Epigenes; and there are the brothers of several who have associated with me. There is Nicostratus the son of Theosdotides, and the brother of Theodotus (now Theodotus himself is dead, and therefore he, at any rate, will not seek to stop him); and there is Paralus the son of Demodocus, who had a brother Theages; and Adeimantus the son of Ariston, whose brother Plato is present; and Aeantodorus, who is the brother of Apollodorus, whom I also see. I might mention a great many others, some of whom Meletus should have produced as witnesses in the course of his speech; and let him still produce them, if he has forgotten; I will make way for him. And let him say, if he has any testimony of the sort which he can produce. Nay, Athenians, the very opposite is the truth. For all these are ready to witness on behalf of the corrupter, of the destroyer of their kindred, as Meletus and Anytus call me; not the corrupted youth only—there might have been a motive for that—but their uncorrupted elder relatives. Why should they too support me with their testimony? Why, indeed, except for the sake of truth and justice, and because they know that I am speaking the truth, and that Meletus is lying.

Well, Athenians, this and the like of this is all the defense which I have to offer. Yet a word more. Perhaps there may be someone who is offended at me, when hu calls to mind how hu humself on a similar, or even a less serious occasion, had recourse to prayers and supplications with many tears, and how hu produced hus children in court, which was a moving spectacle, together with a posse of his relations and friends; whereas I, who am probably in danger of my life, will do none of these things. Perhaps this may come into hus mind, and hu may be set against me, and vote in anger because hu is displeased at this.

Now, if there be such a person among you, which I am far from affirming, I may fairly reply to hum: *My friend, I am a man, and like other men, a creature of flesh and blood, and not of wood or stone, as Homer says*; and I have a family, yes, and sons, O Athenians, three in number, one of whom is growing up, and the two others are still young; and yet I will not bring any of them here in order to petition you for an acquittal. And why not? Not from any self-will or disregard of you. Whether I am or am not afraid of death is another question, of which I will not now speak. But my reason simply is, that I feel such conduct to be discreditable to myself, and you, and the whole state. One who has reached my years, and who has a name for wisdom, whether deserved or not, ought not to demean humself. At any rate, the world has decided that Socrates is in some way superior to other people. And if those among you who are said to be superior in wisdom and courage, and any other virtue, demean themselves in this way, how shameful is their conduct! I have seen persons of reputation, when they have been condemned, behaving in the strangest manner: they seemed to fancy that they were going to suffer something dreadful if they died, and that they could be immortal if you only allowed them to live; and I think they were a dishonor to the state, and that any stranger coming in would say of them that the most eminent people of Athens, to whom the Athenians themselves give honor and command, are no better than housewives.

And I say that these things ought not to be done by those of us who are of reputation; and if they are done, you ought not to permit them; you ought rather to show that you are more inclined to condemn, not the person who is quiet, but the person who gets up a doleful scene and makes the city ridiculous.

But, setting aside the question of dishonor, there seems to be something wrong in petitioning a judge, and thus procuring an acquittal, instead of informing and convincing hum. For hus duty is, not to make a present of justice, but to give judgment; and hu has sworn that hu will judge according to the laws, and not according to hus own good pleasure; and neither hu nor we should get into the habit of perjuring ourselves—there can be no piety in that.

Do not then require me to do what I consider dishonorable and impious and wrong, especially now, when I am being tried for impiety on the indictment of Meletus. For if, people of Athens, by force of persuasion and entreaty, I could overpower your oaths, then I should be teaching you to believe that there are no gods, and convict myself, in my own defense, of not believing in them. But that is not the case; for I do believe that there are gods, and in a far higher sense than that in which any of my accusers believe in them. And to you and to God I commit my cause, to be determined by you as is best for you and me.

●

THERE ARE MANY REASONS WHY I am not grieved, O people of Athens, at the vote of condemnation. I expected this, and am only surprised that the votes are so nearly equal; for I had thought that the majority against me would have been far larger; but now, had thirty votes gone over to the other side, I should have been acquitted. And I may say that I have escaped Meletus. And I may say more; for without the assistance of Anytus and Lycon, he would not have had a fifth part of the votes, as the law requires, in which case he would have incurred a fine of a thousand drachmae, as is evident.

And so he proposes death as the penalty. And what shall I propose on my part, O people of Athens? Clearly that which is my due. And what is that which I ought to pay or to receive? What shall be done to the man who has never had the wit to be idle during his whole life; but has been careless of what the many care about—wealth, and family interests, and military offices, and speaking in the assembly, and magistracies, and plots, and parties. Reflecting that I was really too honest a man to follow in this way and live, I did not go where I could do no good to you or to myself; but where I could do the greatest good privately to every one of you, there I went, and sought to persuade everyone among you, that hu must look to humself, and seek virtue and wisdom before hu looks to hus private interests, and look to the state before hu looks to the interests of the state; and that this should be the order which hu observes in all hus actions. What shall be done to such a one? Doubtless some good thing, O people of Athens, if hu has hus reward; and the good should be of a kind suitable to hum. What would be a reward suitable to a poor fellow who is your benefactor, who desires leisure that he may instruct you? There can be no more fitting reward than maintenance in the prytaneum, O people of Athens, a reward which he deserves far more than the citizen who has won the prize at Olympia in the horse or chariot race, whether the chariots were drawn by two horses or by many. For I am in want, and hu has enough; and hu only gives you the appearance of happiness, and I give you the reality. And if I am to estimate the penalty justly, I say that maintenance in the prytaneum is the just return.

Perhaps you think that I am braving you in saying this, as in what I said before about the tears and prayers. But that is not the case. I speak rather because I am convinced that I never intentionally wronged anyone, although I cannot convince you of that—for we have had a short conversation only; but if there were a law at Athens, such as there is in other cities, that a capital cause should not be decided in one day, then I believe that I should have convinced you; but now the time is too short. I cannot in a moment refute great slanders; and, as I am convinced that I never wronged another, I will assuredly not wrong myself. I will not say of myself that I deserve any evil, or propose any penalty. Why should I? Because I am afraid of the penalty of death which Meletus proposes? When I do not know whether death is a good or an evil, why should I propose a penalty which would certainly be an evil? Shall I say imprisonment? And why should I live in prison, and be the slave of the magistrates of the year—of the Eleven?

Or shall the penalty be a fine, and imprisonment until the fine is paid? There is the same objection. I should have to lie in prison, for money I have none, and cannot pay. And if I say exile (and this may possibly be the penalty which you will affix), I must indeed be blinded by the love of life, if I were to consider that when you, who are my own citizens, cannot endure my discourses and words, and have found them so grievous and odious that you would have done with them, others are likely to endure me. No indeed, people of Athens, that is not very likely.

And what a life should I lead, at my age, wandering from city to city, living in ever-changing exile, and always being driven out! For I am quite sure that into whatever place I go, as here so also there, the young people will come to me; and if I drive them away, their elders will drive me out at their desire; and if I let them come, their fathers and friends will drive me out for their sakes.

Someone will say: *Yes, Socrates, but cannot you hold your tongue, and then you may go into a foreign city, and no one will interfere with you?* Now I have great difficulty in making you understand my answer to this. For if I tell you that this would be a disobedience to a divine command, and therefore that I cannot hold my tongue, you will not believe that I am serious; and if I say again that the greatest human good is daily to converse about virtue, and all that concerning which you hear me examining myself and others, and that the life which is unexamined is not worth living—that you are still less likely to believe.

And yet I say what is true, although a thing of which it is hard for me to persuade you. Moreover, I am not accustomed to think that I deserve any punishment. Had I money I might have proposed to give you what I had, and had been none the worse. But you see that I have none, and can only ask you to proportion the fine to my means. However, I think that I could afford a mina, and therefore I propose that penalty: Plato, Crito, Critobulus, and Apollodorus, my friends here, bid me say thirty minae, and they will be the sureties. Well, then, say thirty minae, let that be the penalty; for that they will be ample security to you.

●

NOT MUCH TIME WILL BE GAINED, O Athenians, in return for the evil name which you will get from the detractors of the city, who will say that you killed Socrates, a wise man; for they will call me wise, even though I am not wise, when they want to reproach you.

If you had waited a little while, your desire would have been fulfilled in the course of nature. For I am far advanced in years, as you may perceive, and not far from death. I am speaking now only to those of you who have condemned me to death.

And I have another thing to say to them: *You think that I was convicted through deficiency of words—I mean, that if I had thought fit to leave nothing undone, nothing unsaid, I might have gained an acquittal.* Not so; the deficiency which led to my conviction was not of words—certainly not. But I had not the boldness or impudence or inclination to address you as you would have liked me to address you, weeping and wailing and lamenting, and saying and doing many things which you have been accustomed to hear from others, and which, as I say, are unworthy of me.

But I thought that I ought not to do anything common or mean in the hour of danger: nor do I now repent of the manner of my defense, and I would rather die having spoken after my manner, than speak in your manner and live. For neither in war nor yet at law ought anyone to use every way of escaping death. For often in battle there is no doubt that if a soldier will throw away hus arms, and fall on hus knees before hus pursuers, hu may escape death; and in other dangers there are other ways of escaping death, if a person is willing to say and do anything. The difficulty, my friends, is not in avoiding death, but in avoiding unrighteousness; for that runs faster than death. I am old and move slowly, and the slower runner has overtaken me, and my accusers are keen and quick, and the faster runner, who is unrighteousness, has overtaken them.

And now I depart hence condemned by you to suffer the penalty of death, and they too go their ways condemned by the truth to suffer the penalty of villainy and wrong; and I must abide by my award—let them abide by theirs. I suppose that these things may be regarded as fated—and I think that they are well.

And now, O people who have condemned me, I would prophesy to you; for I am about to die, and that is the hour in which persons are gifted with prophetic power. And I prophesy to you who are my murderers, that immediately after my death punishment far heavier than you have inflicted on me will surely await you. Me you have killed because you wanted to escape the accuser, and not to give an account of your lives. But that will not be as you suppose: far otherwise. For I say that there will be more accusers of you than there are now; accusers whom hitherto I have restrained: and as they are younger they will be more severe with you, and you will be more offended at them. For if you think that by killing men you can avoid the accuser censuring your lives, you are mistaken; that is not a way of escape which is either possible or honorable; the easiest and the noblest way is not to be crushing others, but to be improving yourselves. This is the prophecy which I utter before my departure to the judges who have condemned me.

Friends, who would have acquitted me, I would like also to talk with you about this thing which has happened, while the magistrates are busy, and before I go to the place at which I must die. Stay then a while, for we may as well talk with one another while there is time. You are my friends, and I should like to show you the meaning of this event which has happened to me. O my judges—for you I may truly call judges—I should like to tell you of a wonderful circumstance. Hitherto the familiar oracle within me has constantly been in the habit of opposing me even about trifles, if I was going to make a slip or error about anything; and now as you see there has come upon me that which may be thought, and is generally believed to be, the last and worst evil. But the oracle made no sign of opposition, either as I was leaving my house and going out in the morning, or when

I was going up into this court, or while I was speaking, at anything which I was going to say; and yet I have often been stopped in the middle of a speech, but now in nothing I either said or did touching this matter has the oracle opposed me. What do I take to be the explanation of this? I will tell you. I regard this as a proof that what has happened to me is a good, and that those of us who think that death is an evil are in error. This is a great proof to me of what I am saying, for the customary sign would surely have opposed me had I been going to evil and not to good.

Let us reflect in another way, and we shall see that there is great reason to hope that death is a good; for one of two things: either death is a state of nothingness and utter unconsciousness, or, as people say, there is a change and migration of the soul from this world to another.

Now, if you suppose that there is no consciousness, but a sleep like the sleep of hum who is undisturbed even by the sight of dreams, death will be an unspeakable gain. For if a person were to select the night in which hus sleep was undisturbed even by dreams, and were to compare with this the other days and nights of his life, and then were to tell us how many days and nights hu had passed in the course of hus life better and more pleasantly than this one, I think that anyone, I will not say a private person, but even the great king will not find many such days or nights, when compared with the others. Now if death is like this, I say that to die is gain; for eternity is then only a single night. But if death is the journey to another place, and there, as people say, all the dead are, what good, O my friends and judges, can be greater than this? If indeed when the pilgrim arrives in the world below, hu is delivered from the professors of justice in this world, and finds the true judges who are said to give judgment there, Minos and Rhadamanthus and Aeacus and Triptolemus, and other children of God who were righteous in their own life, that pilgrimage will be worth making.

What would not a person give if hu might converse with Orpheus and Musaeus and Hesiod and Homer? No, if this be true, let me die again and again. I, too, shall have a wonderful interest in a place where I can converse with Palamedes, and Ajax the son of Telamon, and other heroes of old, who have suffered death through an unjust judgment; and there will be no small pleasure, as I think, in comparing my own sufferings with theirs. Above all, I shall be able to continue my search into true and false knowledge; as in this world, so also in the next; I shall find out who is wise, and who pretends to be wise, and is not. What would not a fellow give, O judges, to be able to examine the leader of the great Trojan expedition; or Odysseus or Sisyphus, or numberless others, men and women too! What infinite delight would there be in conversing with them and asking them questions! For in that world they do not put a person to death for this; certainly not. For besides being happier in that world than in this, they will be immortal, if what is said is true.

Wherefore, O judges, be of good cheer about death, and know this of a truth—that no evil can happen to a good person, either in life or after death. Hu and hus are not neglected by the gods; nor has my own approaching end happened by mere chance.

But I see clearly that to die and be released was better for me; and therefore the oracle gave no sign. For which reason, also, I am not angry with my accusers or my condemners; they have done me no harm, although neither of them meant to do me any good; and for this I may gently blame them.

Still, I have a favor to ask of them. When my sons are grown up, I would ask you, O my friends, to punish them; and I would have you trouble them, as I have troubled you, if they seem to care about riches, or anything, more than about virtue; or if they pretend to be something when they are really nothing—then reprove them, as I have reproved you, for not caring about that for which they ought to care, and thinking that they are something when they are really nothing. And if you do this, both I and my sons will have received justice at your hands.

The hour of departure has arrived, and we go our ways—I to die, and you to live. Which is better God only knows.

●

CRITO

Characters: Socrates, Crito
Scene: The prison of Socrates

SOCRATES: WHY HAVE YOU COME AT THIS HOUR, CRITO? IT MUST be quite early.

CRITO: Yes, certainly.

Soc.: What is the exact time?

CR.: The dawn is breaking.

Soc.: I wonder the keeper of the prison would let you in.

CR.: He knows me because I often come, Socrates; moreover, I have done him a kindness.

Soc.: And are you only just come?

CR.: No, I came some time ago.

Soc.: Then why did you sit and say nothing, instead of awakening me at once?

CR.: Why, indeed, Socrates, I myself would rather not have all this sleeplessness and sorrow. But I have been wondering at your peaceful slumbers, and that was the reason why I did not awaken you, because I wanted you to be out of pain. I have always thought you happy in the calmness of your temperament; but never did I see the like of the easy, cheerful way in which you bear this calamity.

Soc.: Why, Crito, when a person has reached my age hu ought not to be repining at the prospect of death.

CR.: And yet other old people find themselves in similar misfortunes, and age does not prevent them from repining.

Soc.: That may be. But you have not told me why you come at this early hour.

CR.: I come to bring you a message which is sad and painful; not, as I believe, to yourself, but to all of us who are your friends, and saddest of all to me.

Soc.: What? I suppose that the ship has come from Delos, on the arrival of which I am to die?

CR.: No, the ship has not actually arrived, but she will probably be here today, as persons who have come from Sunium tell me that they left her there; and therefore tomorrow, Socrates, will be the last day of your life.

Soc.: Very well, Crito; if such is the will of God, I am willing; but my belief is that there will be a delay of a day.

CR.: Why do you say this?

Soc.: I will tell you. I am to die on the day after the arrival of the ship?

CR.: Yes; that is what the authorities say.

Soc.: But I do not think that the ship will be here until tomorrow; this I gather from a vision which I had last night, or rather only just now, when you fortunately allowed me to sleep.

CR.: And what was the nature of the vision?

Soc.: There came to me the likeness of a woman, fair and comely, clothed in white raiment, who called to me and said: *O Socrates, "The third day hence, to fertile Phthia shall you go."* [Homer, *Iliad*]

CR.: What a singular dream, Socrates!

Soc.: There can be no doubt about the meaning, Crito, I think.

CR.: Yes; the meaning is only too clear. But, O! my beloved Socrates, let me entreat you once more to take my advice and escape. For if you die I shall not only lose a friend who can never be replaced, but there is another evil: people who do not know you and me will believe that I might have saved you if I had been willing to give money, but that I did not care. Now, can there be a worse disgrace than this—that I should be thought to value money more than the life of a friend? For the many will not be persuaded that I wanted you to escape, and that you refused.

Soc.: But why, my dear Crito, should we care about the opinion of the many? Good people, and they are the only persons who are worth considering, will think of these things truly as they happened.

CR.: But do you see, Socrates, that the opinion of the many must be regarded, as is evident in your own case, because they can do the very greatest evil to anyone who has lost their good opinion.

Soc.: I only wish, Crito, that they could; for then they could also do the greatest good, and that would be well. But the truth is, that they can do neither good nor evil: they cannot make a person either wise or make hum foolish; and whatever they do is the result of chance.

CR.: Well, I will not dispute about that; but please to tell me, Socrates, whether you are not acting out of regard to me and your other friends: are you not afraid that if you escape hence we may get into trouble with the informers for having stolen you away, and lose either the whole or a great part of our property; or that even a worse evil may happen to us? Now, if this is your fear, be at ease; for in order to save you, we ought surely to run this, or even a greater risk; be persuaded, then, and do as I say.

Soc.: Yes, Crito, that is one fear which you mention, but by no means the only one.

Cr.: Fear not. There are persons who at no great cost are willing to save you and bring you out of prison; and as for the informers, you may observe that they are far from being exorbitant in their demands; a little money will satisfy them. My means, which, as I am sure, are ample, are at your service, and if you have a scruple about spending all mine, here are strangers who will give you the use of theirs; and one of them, Simmias the Theban, has brought a sum of money for this very purpose; and Cebes and many others are willing to spend their money too.

I say, therefore, do not on that account hesitate about making your escape, and do not say, as you did in the court, that you will have a difficulty in knowing what to do with yourself if you escape. For people will love you in other places to which you may go, and not in Athens only; there are friends of mine in Thessaly, if you like to go to them, who will value and protect you, and no Thessalian will give you any trouble. Nor can I think that you are justified, Socrates, in betraying your own life when you might be saved; this is playing into the hands of your enemies and destroyers; and moreover I should say that you were betraying your children; for you might bring them up and educate them; instead of which you go away and leave them, and they will have to take their chance; and if they do not meet with the usual fate of orphans, there will be small thanks to you. No one should bring children into the world who is unwilling to persevere to the end in their nurture and education.

But you are choosing the easier part, as I think, not the better and manlier, which would rather have become one who professes virtue in all hus actions, like yourself. And, indeed, I am ashamed not only of you, but of us who are your friends, when I reflect that this entire business of yours will be attributed to our want of courage.

The trial need never have come on, or might have been brought to another issue; and the end of all, which is the crowning absurdity, will seem to have been permitted by us, through cowardice and baseness, who might have saved you, as you might have saved yourself, if we had been good for anything (for there was no difficulty in escaping); and we did not see how disgraceful, Socrates, and also miserable all this will be to us as well as to you. Make your mind up then, or rather have your mind already made up, for the time of deliberation is over, and there is only one thing to be done, which must be done, if at all, this very night, and which any delay will render all but impossible; I beseech you therefore, Socrates, to be persuaded by me, and to do as I say.

Soc.: Dear Crito, your zeal is invaluable, if a right one; but if wrong, the greater the zeal the greater the evil; and therefore we ought to consider whether these things shall be done or not. For I am and always have been one of those natures who must be guided by reason, whatever the reason may be which upon reflection appears to me to be the best; and now that this fortune has come upon me, I cannot put away the reasons which I have before given: the principles which up to now I have honored and revered I still honor, and unless we can find other and better principles on the instant, I am certain not to agree with you; no, not even if the power of the multitude could inflict many more imprisonments, confiscations, deaths, frightening us like children with hobgoblin terrors.

But what will be the fairest way of considering the question? Shall I return to your old argument about the opinions of people? some of which are to be regarded, and others, as we were saying, are not to be regarded. Now, were we right in maintaining this before I was condemned? And has the argument which was once good now proved to be talk for the sake of talking; in fact an amusement only, and altogether vanity?

That is what I want to consider with your help, Crito: whether, under my present circumstances, the argument appears to be in any way different or not; and is to be allowed by me or disallowed. That argument, which, as I believe, is maintained by many who assume to be authorities, was to the effect, as I was saying, that the opinions of some people are to be regarded, and of other people not to be regarded. Now you, Crito, are a disinterested person who are not going to die tomorrow—at least, there is no human probability of this, and you are therefore not liable to be deceived by the circumstances in which you are placed. Tell me, then, whether I am right in saying that some opinions, and the opinions of some people only, are to be valued, and other opinions, and the opinions of other people, are not to be valued. I ask you whether I was right in maintaining this?

Cr.: Certainly.

Soc.: The good are to be regarded, and not the bad?

Cr.: Yes.

Soc.: And the opinions of the wise are good, and the opinions of the unwise are evil?

Cr.: Certainly.

Soc.: And what was said about another matter? Was the disciple in gymnastics supposed to attend to the praise and blame and opinion of everyone, or of one person only—hus physician or trainer, whoever that was?

Cr.: Of one person only.

Soc.: And hu ought to fear the censure and welcome the praise of that one only, and not of the many?

Cr.: That is clear.

Soc.: And hu ought to live and train, and eat and drink in the way which seems good to hus single master who has understanding, rather than according to the opinion of all other people put together?

Cr.: True.

Soc.: And if hu disobeys and disregards the opinion and approval of the one, and regards the opinion of the many who have no understanding, will hu not suffer evil?

Cr.: Certainly hu will.

Soc.: And what will the evil be, whither tending and what affecting, in the disobedient person?

Cr.: Clearly, affecting the body; that is what is destroyed by the evil.

Soc.: Very good; and is not this true, Crito, of other things which we need not separately enumerate? In the matter of just and unjust, fair and foul, good and evil, which are the subjects of our present consultation, ought we to follow the opinion of the many and to fear them; or the opinion of the one person who has understanding, and whom we ought to fear and reverence more than all the rest of the world: and whom deserting we shall destroy and injure that principle in us which may be assumed to be improved by justice and deteriorated by injustice; is there such a principle?

Cr.: Certainly there is, Socrates.

Soc.: Take a parallel instance: if, acting under the advice of those who have no understanding, we destroy that which is improved by health and deteriorated by disease—when that has been destroyed, I say, would life be worth having? And that is—the body?

Cr.: Yes.

Soc.: Could we live, having an evil and corrupted body?

Cr.: Certainly not.

Soc.: And will life be worth having, if that higher part of a person be depraved, which is improved by justice and deteriorated by injustice? Do we suppose that principle, whatever it may be in a person, which has to do with justice and injustice, to be inferior to the body?

Cr.: Certainly not.

Soc.: More honored, then?

Cr.: Far more honored.

Soc.: Then, my friend, we must not regard what the many say of us: but what hu, the one person who has understanding of just and unjust, will say, and what the truth will say. And therefore you begin in error when you advise that we should regard the opinion of the many about just and unjust, good and evil, honorable and dishonorable. *Well,* someone will say, *but the many can kill us.*

Cr.: Yes, Socrates; that will clearly be the answer.

Soc.: That is true: but still I find with surprise that the old argument is, as I conceive, unshaken as ever. And I should like to know whether I may say the same of another proposition—that not life, but a good life, is to be chiefly valued?

Cr.: Yes, that also remains.

Soc.: And a good life is equivalent to a just and honorable one—that holds also?

Cr.: Yes, that holds.

Soc.: From these premises I proceed to argue the question whether I ought or ought not to try and escape without the consent of the Athenians: and if I am clearly right in escaping, then I will make the attempt; but if not, I will abstain. The other considerations which you mention, of money and loss of character and the duty of educating children, are, as I fear, only the doctrines of the multitude, who would be as ready to call people to life, if they were able, as they are to put them to death—and with as little reason.

But now, since the argument has thus far prevailed, the only question which remains to be considered is, whether we shall do rightly either in escaping or in suffering others to aid in our escape and paying them in money and thanks, or whether we shall not do rightly; and if the latter, then death or any other calamity which may ensue on my remaining here must not be allowed to enter into the calculation.

Cr.: I think that you are right, Socrates; how then shall we proceed?

Soc.: Let us consider the matter together, and do you either refute me if you can, and I will be convinced; or else cease, my dear friend, from repeating to me that I ought to escape against the wishes of the Athenians: for I am extremely desirous to be persuaded by you, but not against my own better judgment. And now please to consider my first position, and do your best to answer me.

Cr.: I will do my best.

Soc.: Are we to say that we are never intentionally to do wrong, or that in one way we ought and in another way we ought not to do wrong, or is doing wrong always evil and dishonorable, as I was just now saying, and as has been already acknowledged by us? Are all our former admissions which were made within a few days to be thrown away? And have we, at our age, been earnestly discoursing with one another all our life long only to discover that we are no better than children? Or are we to rest assured, in spite of the opinion of the many, and in spite of consequences whether better or worse, of the truth of what was then said, that injustice is always an evil and dishonor to hum who acts unjustly? Shall we affirm that?

CR.: Yes.

Soc.: Then we must do no wrong?

CR.: Certainly not.

Soc.: Nor when injured injure in return, as the many imagine; for we must injure no one at all?

CR.: Clearly not.

Soc.: Again, Crito, may we do evil?

CR.: Surely not, Socrates.

Soc.: And what of doing evil in return for evil, which is the morality of the many—is that just or not?

CR.: Not just.

Soc.: For doing evil to another is the same as injuring hum?

CR.: Very true.

Soc.: Then we ought not to retaliate or render evil for evil to anyone, whatever evil we may have suffered from hum. But I would have you consider, Crito, whether you really mean what you are saying. For this opinion has never been held, and never will be held, by any considerable number of persons; and those who are agreed and those who are not agreed upon this point have no common ground, and can only despise one another when they see how widely they differ. Tell me, then, whether you agree with and assent to my first principle, that neither injury nor retaliation nor warding off evil by evil is ever right. And shall that be the premise of our argument? Or do you decline and dissent from this? For this has been of old and is still my opinion; but, if you are of another opinion, let me hear what you have to say. If, however, you remain of the same mind as formerly, I will proceed to the next step.

CR.: You may proceed, for I have not changed my mind.

Soc.: Then I will proceed to the next step, which may be put in the form of a question: Ought a person to do what hu admits to be right, or ought hu to betray the right?

CR.: Hu ought to do what hu thinks right.

Soc.: But if this is true, what is the application? In leaving the prison against the will of the Athenians, do I wrong any? or rather do I not wrong those whom I ought least to wrong? Do I not desert the principles which were acknowledged by us to be just? What do you say?

CR.: I cannot tell, Socrates; for I do not know.

SOC.: Then consider the matter in this way: Imagine that I am about to play truant (you may call the proceeding by any name which you like), and the laws and the government come and interrogate me: *Tell us, Socrates,* they say, *what are you about? are you going by an act of yours to overturn us—the laws, and the whole state, as far as in you lies? Do you imagine that a state can subsist and not be overthrown, in which the decisions of law have no power, but are set aside and overthrown by individuals?* What will be our answer, Crito, to these and the like words? Anyone, and especially a clever rhetorician, will have a good deal to urge about the evil of setting aside the law which requires a sentence to be carried out. and we might reply, *Yes, but the state has injured us and given an unjust sentence.* Suppose I say that?

CR.: Very good, Socrates.

SOC.: *And was that our agreement with you?* the law would say; *or were you to abide by the sentence of the state?* And if I were to express astonishment at their saying this, the law would probably add: *Answer, Socrates, instead of opening your eyes: you are in the habit of asking and answering questions. Tell us what complaint you have to make against us which justifies you in attempting to destroy us and the state? In the first place, did we not bring you into existence? Your father married your mother by our aid and begat you. Say whether you have any objection to urge against those of us who regulate marriage.*
  None, I should reply.
  Or against those of us who regulate the system of nurture and education of children, in which you were trained? Were not the laws, who have the charge of this, right in commanding your father to train you in music and gymnastic?
  Right, I should reply.
  Well, then, since you were brought into the world and nurtured and educated by us, can you deny in the first place that you are our child and slave, as your parents were before you? And if this is true, you are not on equal terms with us; nor can you think that you have a right to do to us what we are doing to you. Would you have any right to strike or revile or do any other evil to a parent or to your master, if you had one, when you have been struck or reviled by hum, or received some other evil at hus hands?—you would not say this? And because we think right to destroy you, do you think that you have any right to destroy us in return, and your country as far as in you lies? Will you, O professor of true virtue, say that you are justified in this? Has a philosopher like you failed to discover that our country is more to be valued and higher and holier far than mother or father or any ancestor, and more to be regarded in the eyes of the gods and of people of understanding? also to

be soothed, and gently and reverently entreated when angry, even more than a parent, and if not persuaded, or if not persuaded, obeyed? And when we are punished by her, whether with imprisonment or stripes, the punishment is to be endured in silence; and if she lead us to wounds or death in battle, there we follow as is right; neither may anyone yield or retreat or leave hus rank, but whether in battle or in a court of law, or in any other place, hu must do what hus city and hus country order hum; or hu must change their view of what is just: and if hu may do no violence to hus father or mother, much less may hu do violence to hus country.

What answer shall we make to this, Crito? Do the laws speak truly, or do they not?

CR.: I think that they do.

SOC.: Then the laws will say: *Consider, Socrates, if this is true, that in your present attempt you are going to do us wrong. For, after having brought you into the world, and nurtured and educated you, and given you and every other citizen a share in every good that we had to give, we further proclaim and give the right to every Athenian, that if hu does not like us when hu has come of age and has seen the ways of the city, and made our acquaintance, hu may go where hu pleases and take hus goods with hum. Any of you who does not like us and the city, and who wants to go to a colony or to any other city, may go where hu likes, and take hus goods with hum.*

But hu who has experience of the manner in which we order justice and administer the state, and still remains, has entered into an implied contract that hu will do as we command hum. And hu who disobeys us is, as we maintain, thrice wrong; first, because in disobeying us hu is disobeying hus parents; secondly, because we are the authors of hus education; thirdly, because hu has made an agreement with us that hu will duly obey our commands; and hu neither obeys them nor convinces us that our commands are wrong; and we do not rudely impose them, but give hum the alternative of obeying or convincing us—that is what we offer, and hu does neither.

These are the sort of accusations to which, as we were saying, you, Socrates, will be exposed if you accomplish your intentions; you, above all other Athenians.

Suppose I ask, why is this? they will justly retort upon me that I above all other people have acknowledged the agreement. *There is clear proof,* they will say, *Socrates, that we and the city were not displeasing to you. Of all Athenians you have been the most constant resident in the city, which, as you never leave, you may be supposed to love. For you never went out of the city either to see the games, except once when you went to the Isthmus, or to any other place unless you were on military service; nor did you travel as other people do. Nor had you any curiosity to know other states or their laws; your affections did not go beyond us and our state; we were your special favorites, and you acquiesced in our government of you; and this is the city in which you begat your children, which is a proof of your satisfaction.*

Moreover, you might, if you had liked, have fixed the penalty at banishment in the course of the trial—the state which refuses to let you go now would have let you go then. But you pretended that you preferred death to exile, and that you were not grieved at death.

And now you have forgotten these fine sentiments, and pay no respect to us the laws, of whom you are the destroyer; and are doing what only a miserable slave would do, running away and turning your back upon the compacts and agreements which you made as a citizen.

And first of all answer this very question: Are we right in saying that you agreed to be governed according to us in deed, and not in word only? Is that true or not? How shall we answer that, Crito? Must we not agree?

CR.: There is no help, Socrates.

SOC.: Then will they not say: *You, Socrates, are breaking the covenants and agreements which you made with us at your leisure, not in any haste or under any compulsion or deception, but having had seventy years to think of them, during which time you were at liberty to leave the city, if we were not to your mind, or if our covenants appeared to you to be unfair.*

You had your choice, and might have gone either to Lacedaemon or Crete, which you often praise for their good government, or to some other Hellenic or foreign State. Whereas you, above all other Athenians, seemed to be so fond of the state, or, in other words, of us its laws (for who would like a state that has no laws?), that you never stirred out of it; the halt, the blind, the maimed were not more stationary in it than you were.

And now you run away and forsake your agreements. Not so, Socrates, if you will take our advice; do not make yourself ridiculous by escaping out of the city.

For just consider, if you transgress and err in this sort of way, what good will you do, either to yourself or to your friends? That your friends will be driven into exile and deprived of citizenship, or will lose their property, is tolerably certain; and you yourself, if you fly to one of the neighboring cities, as, for example, Thebes or Megara, both of which are well governed cities, will come to them as an enemy, Socrates, and their government will be against you, and all patriotic citizens will cast an evil eye upon you as a subverter of the laws, and you will confirm in the minds of the judges the justice of their own condemnation of you.

For hu who is a corrupter of the laws is more than likely to be a corrupter of the young and foolish portion of humanity.

Will you then flee from well-ordered cities and virtuous people? and is existence worth having on these terms?

Or will you go to them without shame, and talk to them, Socrates? And what will you say to them? What you say here about virtue and justice and institutions and laws being the best things among people? Would that be decent of you? Surely not.

But if you go away from well-governed States to Crito's friends in Thessaly, where there is great disorder and license, they will be charmed to hear the tale of your escape from prison, set off with ludicrous particulars of the manner in which you were wrapped in a goatskin or some other disguise, and metamorphosed as the fashion of runaways is—that is very likely; but will there be no one to remind you that in your old age you violated the most sacred laws from a miserable desire of a little more life?

Perhaps not, if you keep them in a good temper; but if they are out of temper you will hear many degrading things; you will live, but how?—as the flatterer of all people, and the servant of all people; and doing what?— eating and drinking in Thessaly, having gone abroad in order that you may get a dinner.

And where will be your fine sentiments about justice and virtue then? Say that you wish to live for the sake of your children, that you may bring them up and educate them—will you take them into Thessaly and deprive them of Athenian citizenship? Is that the benefit which you will confer upon them? Or are you under the impression that they will be better cared for and educated here if you are still alive, although absent from them; for that your friends will take care of them? Do you fancy that if you are an inhabitant of Thessaly they will take care of them, and if you an inhabitant of the other world they will not take care of them? No; but if they who call themselves friend are truly friends, they surely will.

Listen, then, Socrates, to us who have brought you up. Think not of life and children first, and of justice afterwards, but of justice first, that you may be justified before the princes of the world below. For neither will you nor any that belong to you be happier or holier or juster in this life, or happier in another, if you do as Crito bids.

Now you depart in innocence, a sufferer and not a doer of evil; a victim, not of the laws, but of people. But if you go forth, returning evil for evil, and injury for injury, breaking the covenants and agreements which you have made with us, and wronging those whom you ought least to wrong, that is to say, yourself, your friends, your country, and us, we shall be angry with you while you live, and our brethren, the laws in the world below, will receive you as an enemy; for they will know that you have done your best to destroy us. Listen, then, to us and not to Crito.

This is the voice which I seem to hear murmuring in my ears, like the sound of the flute in the ears of the mystic; that voice, I say, is humming in my ears, and prevents me from hearing any other. And I know that anything more which you may say will be vain. Yet speak, if you have anything to say.

Cr.: I have nothing to say, Socrates.

Soc.: Then let me follow the intimations of the will of God.

●